YOUR PURPOSE IS YOUR SUPERPOWER

Discover Your Life's Assignment
And Become A Powerful You

WORKBOOK

From Best Selling Author

HENRY L. RAZOR

Your Purpose is Your Superpower (The Workbook)
Discover Your life's Assignment and Become A Powerful You
Copyright © 2023 by Henry L. Razor

This workbook is developed to be used with the book "Your Purpose is Your Superpower."

For information contact:

www.shepublishingllc.com or info@shepublishingllc.com

www.fpbi.net

Cover and Title Page Design by Michelle Hudson

ISBN: 978-1-953163-69-1 (workbook)

First Edition: May 2023

10 9 8 7 6 5 4 3 2 1

S.H.E. PUBLISHING, LLC

Objectives

This workbook is produced and intended to accompany the '***Your Purpose is Your Superpower***' book. It can be effectively used in workshop, conferences, and seminars. Although the process and procedures outlined in this book have a history of effectiveness and success, no guarantee is made pertaining to the usage and application of these principles because personal adherence to and compliance with these guidelines and principles are not assessed, validated, or verified; neither is there ever any attempt to assess, validate, or verify. Faith varies and is individual and personal, and as such, so are the results of applying the principles of this workbook.

At the completion of this workbook, the participant should be able to

- State why knowing your purpose is critical for life's success
- List three ways in which we discover our purpose
- Apply the content and biblical structure presented in this seminar to your life to arrive at what God has placed you on this earth to do

Outline

- Purpose Defined -- The reason spiritual warfare exists
- Your God Appointed Purpose comes from God
- Three avenues for discovering your purpose
  - When God clearly informs you of your purpose
  - When you must discover your purpose through life's work & achievements
  - When your purpose is thrust upon you
- The Purpose Discovery activity and exercise

Workbook Functional Key

Q. -- General Question

Qd. – Question for discussion

D – Topic for discussion after reading. Discussion should focus on identifying how the lesson of the topic can best be applied to your personal experience.

A – Activity to be worked through (*with discussion if it is being performed as a team activity*)

E – Exercise to be performed

What is Purpose

Understanding what God has placed you on earth to do provides you with the foundation for success in life's endeavors. When you know that you have taken the correct path, you have increased confidence in your daily walk as well as increased motivation when confronting challenges and obstacles that may stand between you and your final destination.

Proverbs 19:21 KJV

There are many devices in a man's heart;
Nevertheless the counsel of the LORD, that shall stand.

ESV
Many are the plans in the mind of a man, but it is the purpose of
the Lord that will stand.

Qd. What were your life plans as a youth? Are you currently doing what you planned to do as a youth?

Purpose

Purpose - the reason for which something exists or is done, made, used, etc.[1]

Purpose provides us with the reason that God placed us here on earth.

Q. Who makes all purpose assignments?

_____

_____

_____

Let's begin by making this personal. Your purpose is the reason why you are here! It's the reason that you exist on the face of the earth. It is the reason for your very being.

Q. What is it that you think God placed you on earth to do?

_____

_____

_____

_____

_____

_____

---

[1] Dictionary.com

Q. What are the two requirements for successfully fulfilling our purpose and explain why?

_____

_____

_____

_____

_____

_____

_____

_____

_____

_____

Qd. When we function within our area of purpose, we don't compete with each other, but rather we acquire understanding of how the assignments of others complement and enhance our work, and vice-versa. List some of the ways that your area of purpose inter-relates to the purpose area of others

_____

_____

_____

_____

Qd. When considering Divine Purpose, how can the role of God be similar to the responsibilities of a Project Manager

_____

_____

_____

_____

Q. At what time was your Divine Purpose assigned to you and what verse in Ephesians supports your answer?

_____

_____

_____

_____

Q. What two objects of your faith is necessary for successful completion of your purpose?

_____

_____

_____

_____

Qd. How does Philippians 4:13 relate to fulfillment of your purpose?

_____

_____

_____

_____

NOTES

Everyone has Purpose

Q. What happened to Adam and Eve that caused them to be re-directed away from their Divine Purpose?

_____

_____

_____

_____

Q. What was the assignment that God issued to Israel?

_____

_____

_____

_____

Qd. When God made Man, His plan was to establish His Kingdom on earth like it is in heaven. What caused His plan to be delayed? Explain and give scripture references?

_____

_____

_____

_____

_____

_____

_____

_____

Qd. Are all Divine Purposes related to religion, the church, or the temple?

☐ Yes -- Please explain

_____

_____

_____

_____

☐ No -- Please explain

_____

_____

_____

_____

Q. What percentage of the nation of Israel had purposes that were directly related to religious functions?

_____

_____

_____

_____

Q. In Ephesians 4:1, what is the Apostle Paul emphasizing?

_____

_____

_____

_____

Q. If Israel is to function as the priests for the world as the Bible stated, then what percentage of the world would have Divine Assignments that are not directly related to religion, the church, or the temple?

_____

_____

_____

_____

Qd. Why are all purposes divine?

_____

_____

_____

_____

We could go to the ministerial callings and positions of help and support in the church, but your God given purpose may not even be within the confines of religion. The reason this is true because the mission of the church is to be the salt of the world.[2]

---

[2] Matthew 5:13-20

So your God assigned purpose that improves the world may have you serving humanity and mankind from areas that are not associated with religion. Your purpose could be teaching, or banking, or inventing, running a social services Non Profit, athletics, entertaining, or one of numerous functions on earth.

What ever that purpose is, if it is assigned by God then it is for the benefit of all humanity.

NOTES

The Purpose Discovery Process

Qd. Your purpose was defined by God before your birth. How were the conditions of your arrival by birth relative to your purpose?

_____

_____

_____

_____

Q. What does **predestination** mean?

_____

_____

_____

_____

_____

_____

Q. Is everyone predestined to fulfill their divine purpose and go to heaven? What biblical scriptures support your answer to this question?

_____

_____

_____

_____

_____

List the three ways that our life's purpose is discovered

1.

_____

_____

2.

_____

_____

3.

_____

_____

Purpose Identified at Birth

(D)

This is probably the easiest and simplest way to determine your life's purpose. God informs the parents, who begin preparation for the child even before they enter into this world. We have clear examples of this in the bible.

Samson

Judges13:2-5

> 2. And there was a certain man of Zorah, of the family of the Danites, whose name *was* Manoah; and his wife *was* barren, and bare not.
>
> 3. And the angel of the LORD appeared unto the woman, and said unto her, Behold now, thou *art* barren, and bearest not: but thou shalt conceive, and bear a son.
>
> 4. Now therefore beware, I pray thee, and drink not wine nor strong drink, and eat not any unclean *thing:*
>
> 5. for, lo, thou shalt conceive, and bear a son; and no razor shall come on his head: for the child shall be a Nazarite unto God from the womb: and he shall begin to deliver Israel out of the hand of the Philistines.

It is clearly stated here that God sends an angel to the parents of Samson to announce his birth. They are given strict guidelines for themselves in preparation of his birth, and the reason for these strict guidelines is the purpose of the child. In the fifth verse, Samson's purpose in life is set forth by the angel. His purpose was ***"begin to deliver Israel out of the hand of the Philistines."*** Samson's existence on earth was to start the delivering of Israel from the oppressive and abusive power of the Philistines.

The story of Samson's purpose highlights more than anything else, that God has a complete and thorough plan for humanity in the earth. Samson was birthed into this earth with a mission to defeat the Philistines. And even though his focus was the defeat the Philistines, any victory he won or advancements he made would only be the beginning of the enemy's defeat. God could have instantly put down the Philistines, but He didn't. His plan for their defeat spanned hundreds of years and included numerous individuals. We see that what Samson started, David finished.[3]

Sometimes it appears that even though you are doing well in the fight, the obstacles and opposition still aren't going away. But stay focused in your purpose walk because you are only responsible for the part of the plan assigned to you by God. God has other individuals assigned to other areas, and you all may be in the same war, but on different battlefronts and fighting during different time periods. The mission that God has purposed for you may not be complete for generations, so be encouraged and motivated.

---

[3] 2 Samuel 21:15-22

Jeremiah

Jeremiah 1:4-5

> 4. Then the word of the LORD came unto me, saying,
>
> 5. Before I formed thee in the belly I knew thee; and before thou camest forth out of the womb I sanctified thee, *and* I ordained thee a prophet unto the nations

With Jeremiah we see a situation that is similar to Samson's but yet different. Jeremiah is a young man when the Lord appeared to him and announced his life's purpose. It has been estimated that he was between 16-22 years old at the time. Although he was not a baby, or toddler, he was yet young and the majority of years in his life were in front of him.

It is at this early age that God announces his purpose. God emphasizes to Jeremiah that his purpose was set before he was impregnated in his mother's womb (**before the foundations of the world**). We are not informed as to whether his parents were aware of his purpose as Samson's parents were, or if they were given any special instructions to prepare him for his purpose as Samson's parents were, but the fact that God informed him directly at birth that his life's purpose was set also speaks to God's master plan for the world.

Since Jeremiah's father, Hilkiah, was a priest, he would have been in alignment with God. Therefore, it's not a reach to conclude that the knowledge of his life's purpose was known to his parents.

So with Samson, Jeremiah, and others that had their purpose identified at birth or early in life, God aligned parents played a critical and key role in this knowledge being shared by God. We see this also in the example of

Timothy[4]. Paul indicates that the faith that Timothy possessed was first in his grandmother Lois and his mother Eunice.

In each of the cases where the purpose was identified at birth (or a very early age), there is sufficient evidence of the parents being aligned with God. But even with God aligned parents, it wasn't until the child also came into alignment with God that they became aware of what their life's purpose was.

This is a point that should not be taken lightly.

IF YOU WANT TO KNOW YOUR PURPOSE IN LIFE, YOU NEED TO BE ALIGNED WITH THE ONE THAT MAKES THOSE ASSIGNMENTS. **GOD!**

Alignment with God is the only way to acquire the correct knowledge of your life's purpose!

I opened this section by stating that purpose identification at birth is probably the easiest and simplest way to determine your life's purpose. That being said, it is not the only way, and I dare say, that it is not the way that the majority of people come to grips with their purpose today.

---

[4] 2 Timothy 1:5

NOTES

Purpose Identified through Life's Work and Achievements

(D)

Keep in mind that our focus here is on us discovering our purpose. God knew what He wanted us to do before the foundation of the world.

This is a point that cannot be over emphasized. Since God knows our purpose before we are born, even before the foundations of the earth, then the environment that we enter into at birth can play a major role in discovering our purpose. There are things that are beyond our control, but since God is the one that makes the purpose assignments, and He also controls the universe, He brings us into the world prepping us for our assignment and we don't even realize it. So much of your past was really preparation for your purpose, and you won't realize or understand it until such a time as you begin to walk in your life's purpose. You've learned a lot, you cried a lot, you were often in pain, you got beat up a lot, etc. You didn't understand why this was happening to you or why this was your lot in life until you knew your purpose.

Many that were born into poverty found their purpose in lifting others from poverty. Many that were born into broken families found their purpose in building strong families. Many that were birthed into violent and volatile environments find their purpose helping others achieve safety and peace. And through it all, they never realized that the pain of their past was preparation for walking in their purpose.

The knowledge that God brought you along the path that you traversed to prepare you for your assignment becomes obvious and apparent when you become aligned with God. You may have selected a career because you thought that it would lead to prosperity and great wealth, and it may very well do that, but when you become aligned with God you realize that your career path was planned by God to prepare you for your assignment. You may have decided to relocate because you like a certain area and it is where you want to settle down, only to learn that your relocation was a part of God's plan to bring you to your purpose. If there is one individual in the Bible whose past life's work, achievements, and accomplishments were preparation for his life's purpose, it was the Apostle Paul.

The Apostle Paul

Acts 22:3-4

> 3. I am verily a man *which am* a Jew, born in Tarsus, *a city* in Cilicia, yet brought up in this city at the feet of Gamaliel, *and* taught according to the perfect manner of the law of the fathers, and was zealous toward God, as ye all are this day.

> 4. And I persecuted this way unto the death, binding and delivering into prisons both men and women.

Acts 26:4-5, 9-11

> 4. My manner of life from my youth, which was at the first among mine own nation at Jerusalem, know all the Jews;

> 5. which knew me from the beginning, if they would testify, that after the most straitest sect of our religion I lived a Pharisee

> 9. I verily thought with myself, that I ought to do many things contrary to the name of Jesus of Nazareth.

10. Which thing I also did in Jerusalem: and many of the saints did I shut up in prison, having received authority from the chief priests; and when they were put to death, I gave my voice against *them*.

11. And I punished them oft in every synagogue, and compelled *them* to blaspheme; and being exceedingly mad against them, I persecuted *them* even unto strange cities.

Paul was birthed into a family of elite Jews. He had been raised to be in leadership among his Jewish brethren. He even went as far as imprisoning, persecuting, and murdering Jews that converted to the faith. But once he came into alignment with God, he realized that his past life's work and achievements were God's plan for his life's purpose. He may have thought that the knowledge acquired at the feet of noted teacher Gamaliel was to be used in the hierarchy of Jewish customs, but God planned it to be used to minister to the Gentiles.

Which of the disciples had the knowledge of the Torah that matched Paul's? But when he acquired this knowledge, he thought that he was acquiring this knowledge in his plan to rise among the Pharisees. But God's plan for his acquisition of this knowledge was for him to use it in his God assigned life purpose and he was totally unaware of the reason that God brought him along that path until he came into alignment with God.

If you are searching for your life's purpose, start by:

1. aligning yourself with God as best as you can,
2. performing a thorough audit and assessment of your life from as early as you can to obtain your life's data. Note lessons learned, expertise & skills acquired, life changing/impacting encounters and events,
3. objectively analyze your current skills and expertise to determine the areas where your strongest skill sets abide
4. petition God concerning your strong skill sets as to whether these are the skills that He has given you to use in your purpose
5. until you hear from God, start using the strength of your skill sets to perform work that brings positive impact

You will find that your past has prepared you for the assignment that God has appointed you to. If this is not the case with you, then surely God will re-direct you to your purpose because you are in alignment with him and using your achievements, expertise, knowledge, and skills for good and positive impact.

NOTES

Your Purpose Thrust Upon You

(D)

In a book that I recently read; Napoleon Hill introduced me to what he referred to as the *"other self"*. He indicated that he was introduced to it by Mr. Andrew Carnegie shortly before the great depression of 1929. I immediately understood that what he labeled as the *"other self"*, I correctly referred to as the *"soul"* in my book Winning Spiritual Wars. But he made a very awakening point when referring to the *"other self"*. In his book, he stated that the *"other self"* comes forth at times of unusual emergency, at the times when men are forced, through adversity and temporary defeat, to change their habits and think their way out of adversity. In other words, life will thrust you into situations where you are forced to act, or suffer demise.

It has been said that you never know how strong you are until strength is your only choice for advancement and/or survival.

I've found this to be true for many when discovering their purpose. They were believers that were seeking God, living in obedience to God's word as best they could, and doing good work in church, community, society, etc. But it wasn't until they had to respond to a dire emergency that they found their purpose. Sometimes when I consider individuals that were thrust into their purpose in this manner, I am amazed that they did not know their purpose until confronted with an emergency or catastrophe. But maybe they were so consumed with other areas of life that they failed to recognize God urging them towards their purpose. Or maybe they didn't recognize the voice of God directing them towards their purpose. This was the case with Samuel. God called him multiple times and he didn't recognize the call as God[5]. But thankfully Samuel had Eli to provide sound counsel. We find in life that when confronted with life-or-death situations and all that's available to you is you, you will call upon the knowledge gained in the past, expertise and skills acquired in the past, lesson learned in the past to make it through the current emergency. You may feel unqualified, unprepared, unequipped, or just not able, but you are all that's available and every part of your past experiences becomes tools that only you can use to overcome the obstacles facing you. You then realize that the tools you were equipped with by God were intended to be use for the purpose that He assigned to you in life. Moses was one that had his purpose Thrust upon Him.

Moses

Exodus 3:10-11; 4:10

> 10. Come now therefore, and I will send thee unto Pharaoh, that thou mayest bring forth my people the children of Israel out of Egypt.

> 11. And Moses said unto God, Who *am* I, that I should go unto Pharaoh, and that I should bring forth the children of Israel out of Egypt?

Exodus 4:10

---

[5] 1 Samuel 3:1-15

10. And Moses said unto the LORD, O my Lord, I *am* not eloquent, neither heretofore, nor since thou hast spoken unto thy servant: but I *am* slow of speech, and of a slow tongue.

A reading of the third and fourth chapters of Exodus reveals that Moses gave God numerous reasons why he was not the one that should lead the Israelites out of Egypt. But unbeknownst to him, every detail of his life to very time that God appeared to him in the burning bush[6] had been planned as preparation for his life's purpose.

⇒ Consider the events surrounding the birth of Moses.[7]

⇒ Consider God's placement of Moses as a child and the things he learned about Pharaoh and the Egyptians[8]

⇒ Consider the actions of Moses confronting the aggressive Egyptian[9]

Everything about Moses upbringing and development was centered on his God given purpose and he had no knowledge of this until he was confronted with an emergency.

Sometimes your situation will highlight your purpose as did Moses.

Moses didn't know he had the ability until his ability was all he had to get through his storm. He then realized that this ability was invested in him for the benefit of Israel.

---

[6] Exodus chapters 3 & 4
[7] Exodus chapter 2
[8] Exodus 2:10
[9] Exodus 2:11-15

Our purpose is to serve for the benefit of mankind and the improvement of the world. It is critical that you know and walk in your God appointed purpose because the world is waiting on you and only you can fulfill you purpose.

Remember that the world is waiting for you to do what God placed you on this earth to do. Only you can do it and there are no substitutions or fill ins.

Romans 8:19

[19] For the earnest expectation of the creature waiteth for the manifestation of the sons of God.

NOTES

Purpose Discovery Process (E)

PERFOM THE LIFE'S PURPOSE DISCOVERY EXERCISE

YOU

1st NO — Are you unsure what your Life's Purpose is? — YES → Perform Life's Purpose Discovery Exercise

NO

2nd NO — Was your Life's Purpose Identified by God at Birth or very young age — YES → Implement 'CCC' plan in the appendix of Your Purpose is Your Superpower Book.

NO — Did you Experience a life defining moment and you responded with skills that you already possessed? — YES

NO — Where you successful when you stepped up? — YES

NO — Did you feel satisfied after the event and somewhat shocked at how well equipped you were to handle the situation? — YES → Implement 'CCC' plan in the appendix of Your Purpose is Your Superpower Book.

(A)

Step 1. Alignment with God.

Alignment with God is critical

- I will pray _____ minutes daily asking for God's guidance
- I will read _____ verses from my Bible

Step 2. Life Audit

- My birth date

- Do I believe in and regularly seek divine guidance?

- My highest Level of education

- Additional or specific training acquired

- Three Major challenges to my life since youth

  1) _____

  _____

  _____

  2) _____

  _____

  _____

  3) _____

  _____

  _____

- The outcome of these three major life's challenges

  1) _____

  _____

  _____

  2) _____

  _____

  _____

  3) _____

  _____

  _____

- Was there anything was common about these three challenges?

_____

_____

_____

_____

_____

_____

_____

- In what ways did these three challenges change your life?

_____

_____

_____

_____

_____

_____

_____

- What are the good things that you are still doing today that you started doing to survive these challenges?

_____

_____

_____

_____

_____

_____

_____

These good things are strengths that you acquired on your journey to where you are today. Make a strong mental note, because these strengths were given to you for purpose fulfillment.

Step 3. Skills, Education, and Training Assessment

Q. What was the core concentration of your education centered on? your college major * your college minor * training certifications * specialized training * informal training

_____

_____

_____

_____

_____

_____

_____

_____

Q. What are your three strongest skills?

_____

_____

_____

_____

_____

_____

Q. Are you currently using these skills in your career, community, or church (**CCC**)?

_____

_____

_____

_____

Q. Which of your strongest skills

- o were learned during the challenges of your life

- o were qualified with your education or training

- o and you are using today

If you are a believer and have been seeking divine guidance, you have arrived at your purpose area. The skills that you were forced to acquire and use to survive your challenges, the skills that were strengthened by your education or training, and you continue to use today; these are what you have been divinely guided to for your purpose.

If you are not a believer, then this is not applicable. This activity assumes that the participant believes in a divine purpose giver that is omniscient and has orchestrated a plan for the good of humanity; and included within this plan are the purposes for all of His creation.

Step 4. Seek the Purpose Giver for guidance and the positive opportunities in which to use your skills, your expertise, your strengths, your knowledge, etc. If you are currently not using these skills in your area of purpose, now is the time to get started. Seek the purpose Giver for direction on where or how to best utilize His investment in you is for your good, for the good of the community, and for the good of the world. For this step I direct you to the CCC section in the appendix of **Your Purpose is Your Superpower** book.

Step 5. Start using your skills, your experience, your knowledge, your strengths, etc., for positive activities. You will then be on your way to living your best life!

NOTES

NOTES

NOTES

NOTES

NOTES

www.fpbi.net